THE 12 BIGGEST BREAKTHROUGHS IN
ENERGY TECHNOLOGY

by M. M. Eboch

12
STORY
LIBRARY

www.12StoryLibrary.com

12-Story Library is an imprint of Peterson Publishing Company and Press Room Editions.

Produced for 12-Story Library by Red Line Editorial

Photographs ©: majeczka/Shutterstock Images, cover, 1; Library of Congress, 4, 9; Georgios Kollidas/Shutterstock Images, 5; Jim Parkin/Shutterstock Images, 6; James Jones Jr/Shutterstock Images, 7; Caufield & Shook/Library of Congress, 8; H.C. White Co./Library of Congress, 10; Lee Yiu Tung/Shutterstock Images, 11, 29; Andrey Shchekalev/Shutterstock Images, 12; Aleksei Andreev/Shutterstock Images, 13; SpaceKris/Shutterstock Images, 14; N. Minton/Shutterstock Images, 16, 28; Tsuguliev/Shutterstock Images, 17; Foto by M/Shutterstock Images, 18; manfredxy/Shutterstock Images, 19; LianeM/Shutterstock Images, 20; Anton Foltin/Shutterstock Images, 21; Aliaksei Smalenski/Shutterstock Images, 22; wasanajai/Shutterstock Images, 23; Mopic/Shutterstock Images, 24; risteski goce/Shutterstock Images, 25; Jose Gil/Shutterstock Images, 26; Anglia Press Agency/AP Images, 27

ISBN
978-1-63235-013-8 (hardcover)
978-1-63235-073-2 (paperback)
978-1-62143-054-4 (hosted ebook)

Library of Congress Control Number: 2014937354

Printed in the United States of America
Mankato, MN
June, 2014

Go beyond the book. Get free, up-to-date content on this topic at 12StoryLibrary.com.

TABLE OF CONTENTS

THE STEAM ENGINE POWERS THE INDUSTRIAL REVOLUTION

Humans have always needed sources of power. For most of history, people burned wood, straw, or waste. These were simple sources for heat and light. The first machines also used these fuels. Even early trains burned wood.

Early industries were powered by waterwheels. Flowing water would turn a wheel to create power. In the 1600s, inventors started experimenting with steam power. A steam engine burns coal or wood to heat water. The steam created by the boiling water moves parts in an

This steam engine, made in 1879, was used in a sugar mill in Hawaii.

engine. Thomas Savery patented the first steam-powered pump in 1698. Thomas Newcomen made a more efficient steam-powered pump in 1712. These early pumps were used to remove water from mines.

In 1765, James Watt created a steam-powered engine that needed much less fuel. By the 1800s, steam engines were used to power trains and boats. Boats and trains started carrying passengers as well as goods. People were able to travel great distances more easily. Some factories that had used waterwheels switched

to steam engines. Factories no longer needed to be built next to water. The new power source helped them produce more goods. Steam power helped set off the Industrial Revolution. This period was marked by rapid growth in industries and cities.

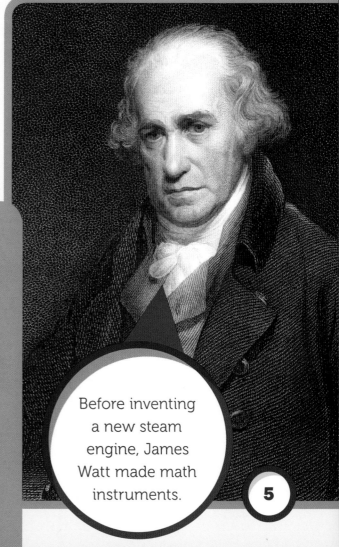

Before inventing a new steam engine, James Watt made math instruments.

1

Number of steam locomotives operating on a major railroad in the United States as of 2012.

- Patented by James Watt in 1769.
- Increased demand for coal as fuel.
- Allowed easy travel.
- Drove the Industrial Revolution.

NEW DRILL IMPROVES ACCESS TO OIL

Oil is a thick, black liquid found underground. In approximately 1855, a chemist named Benjamin Silliman found a way to turn oil into kerosene. Kerosene can be burned in lamps for light. Demand for oil grew quickly, and oil companies dug many wells. But they needed better ways to access the oil.

At first, people dug wells using simple tools, such as shovels. The diggers had to stop often to remove rocks and mud. It could take months to drill a few dozen feet. Some oil deposits are more than 100 feet (30.5 m) deep. Steam power made drilling faster. The early 1900s brought even better ways to drill. A rotary drill has a hollow drill bit. Broken rocks and mud could be washed out of the hole. This meant the drill could work steadily instead of stopping for the removal of rock chips.

Modern oil rigs still use rotary drills. Most are powered by diesel engines.

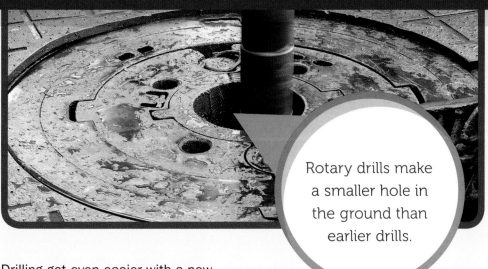

Rotary drills make a smaller hole in the ground than earlier drills.

Drilling got even easier with a new type of drill bit. In 1908, Texas oilman Howard R. Hughes Sr. introduced a bit with two cones that work together. It could drill through much harder rock and work faster. Deeper wells could be dug with the new bit.

18.83 million

Number of barrels of oil used in the United States each day.

- The first rotary drill was invented by Englishman Robert Beart in 1844.
- Rotary drilling was first used for oil in 1901 in Texas.
- Howard R. Hughes Sr. introduced a new drill bit in 1908 in Texas.

Better drilling tools made oil common and cheap. Oil burns cleaner than coal. That means it does not make as much pollution. Oil is also easier to move and store than coal because it is liquid. The use of oil grew quickly. It was used to produce light, heat, and electricity. By 1950, oil had become the United States' most used energy source.

FOSSIL FUELS

Fossil fuels are formed in the earth. They come from plants or animals that died a long time ago. Coal, oil, and natural gas are fossil fuels. These fuels are the most commonly used sources of energy.

GASOLINE ENGINES BRING AGE OF AUTOMOBILES

Automobiles have been around since the 1700s. The first cars had steam engines. These cars were noisy and hard to use. Some cars used electric batteries. They could only go 20 miles (32 km) before needing a charge. These early models were expensive. Not many people were able to use them.

In 1886, Karl Friedrich Benz made what is considered the first true motor car. It had three wheels and a gasoline engine. A gasoline engine uses fuel made from oil. People worried that Benz's car was not reliable. Then his wife drove 62 miles (100 km) with her two sons in one day. This trip got a lot of publicity and showed people that the car was safe.

Rows of Ford Model T cars, the first affordable automobiles, wait to be delivered in 1925.

15 million

Number of Ford Model T cars sold between 1908 and 1927.

- Developed by Karl Friedrich Benz in 1886 in Germany.
- Safer and more reliable than steam-engine cars.
- More efficient than electric cars.
- Increased demand for oil.

RUNNING OUT OF FOSSIL FUELS

The supply of fossil fuels is limited. There is only so much coal, oil, and natural gas under the earth's surface. Some scientists believe we will run out of fossil fuels by 2050. New technologies may help find more oil. But the limited supply has led scientists to search for other fuel sources.

Cars that ran on gasoline were easier to use. They could travel greater distances. They were also less likely to catch fire or explode than cars with steam engines. Demand for cars increased starting in the 1890s. In 1900, fewer than 8,000 families in the United States had cars. By the 1920s, US residents owned more than 8 million cars. All these cars added to the demand for oil to make gasoline.

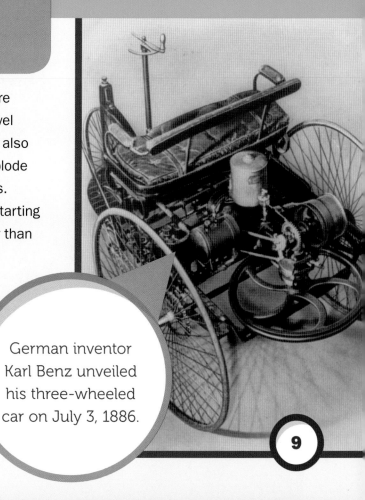

German inventor Karl Benz unveiled his three-wheeled car on July 3, 1886.

EDISON'S LIGHTBULB LEADS TO FIRST POWER STATION

Thomas Edison invented a usable lightbulb in 1879. It was the first electric light source that was safe and efficient enough for widespread use. But it would only be practical if homes and businesses had access to electricity. Edison started working on the idea of a central power station that would supply electricity to nearby buildings. From 1879 to 1882, he built generators. He worked on ways to control the

Edison's first power station used steam engines to turn generators.

500,000

Miles (804,672 km) of power lines in the United States.

- Thomas Edison invented the lightbulb in 1879.
- The first public power plant opened in New York City in 1882.
- Electric lights replaced gas-powered lights.
- By 1950, almost all Americans had electricity.

electricity that would go out through copper wires. Edison opened the world's first public power plant in 1882 in New York City. Soon, more power plants were being built. Early plants couldn't transmit power very far. They supplied power to electric lighting systems in nearby buildings, such as theaters and hotels.

In the early 1900s, power plants became larger and more efficient. They started using alternating-current (AC) technology developed in Europe. This technology let plants provide power from greater distances. In 1907, power companies were outputting 5.9 million kilowatt hours. By 1927, output had risen to 75.4 million kilowatt hours.

Electricity generated by a power station is measured in watts.

TURBINES PRODUCE HYDROELECTRIC POWER

People have used waterwheels to generate power for more than 2,000 years. A flowing river turned the wheel. Gears in the wheel ground grain into flour. Waterwheels could also saw wood and do other tasks. They powered simple factories before the steam engine was invented in the 1700s.

Before the 1800s, water power could not be used far from the water source. Factories had to be built directly on a river. Then inventors figured out how to use water to generate electricity. Most hydroelectric power plants are still built on large rivers. A dam controls the water. Water falls quickly through a tunnel. The moving water turns a turbine. This runs a motor to make electricity. The electricity can then be sent over a wide area through power lines.

Water flowing through the plant turns turbines, which are connected to generators like these.

Hydroelectric plants usually include a dam to control the water flow.

The first hydroelectric power plant began operating in 1882 in Wisconsin. H. J. Rogers started the plant. He was inspired by the power plant built by Thomas Edison in New York. Edison's power plant used steam, but Rogers's plant used the Fox River. At first, it only made enough electricity to light three buildings. Later, hydroelectric plants produced much more power. By 1886, between 40 and 50 hydroelectric plants were working in the United States and Canada.

2,400

Number of hydroelectric dams in the United States as of 2013.

- First used by H. J. Rogers in 1882.
- Provides low-cost electricity.
- Renewable resource.
- Produces little pollution.

RENEWABLE ENERGY

Some forms of energy are renewable. This means the energy is made from a source that does not run out. Once coal and oil are taken from the ground, they are gone. Water, wind, and sunlight are renewable resources.

13

NUCLEAR PLANTS PROVIDE CHEAP, CLEAN ENERGY

Everything in the universe is made of tiny particles called atoms. The core, or nucleus, of each atom contains large amounts of energy. Scientists discovered that splitting atoms releases that energy. In the 1940s, they started trying to figure out ways to use that energy to make electricity.

The world's first nuclear power plant opened in Russia in 1954. In a nuclear power plant, the heat from splitting atoms is used to turn water into steam. The steam turns the blades of a turbine. The turbine spins the generator, and the generator makes electricity.

The large silos at a nuclear power plant are cooling towers. They are full of water to keep the plant cool.

By the twenty-first century, nuclear power plants provided 15 percent of the world's energy. In 2012, more than 400 nuclear reactors were generating electricity in 30 different countries. Nuclear power is popular because it costs less to produce than power from coal or oil. When they are working properly, nuclear power plants also do not cause air pollution. But if something goes wrong, melting fuel rods can release a dangerous energy called radiation into the air. This is called a meltdown. Nuclear plants have many safety measures to prevent radiation from being released. But opponents of nuclear power think the risk is too great.

NUCLEAR WASTE

Nuclear power plants create waste that is radioactive. It is dangerous to people and to the environment. The waste is stored at or near nuclear plants. But with more waste being made, scientists are looking for better long-term solutions. Some want to build storage units underground. But most people do not want nuclear waste stored near them. The question of where to store waste is an ongoing issue with nuclear power.

GEOTHERMAL POWER USES EARTH'S UNDERGROUND HEAT

Geothermal energy comes from heat inside the earth. This heat is held inside rocks and water underground. In some places, the heat may be close to the ground surface. These areas often have hot springs or volcanoes. People have used this natural heat for cooking and heating for thousands of years.

Geothermal power can also be used to make electricity. Steam from the hot water turns turbines, and the turbines run a generator. An Italian businessman first tried this in 1904 in Italy. Piero Ginori Conti used steam coming from the ground to turn a small turbine. He was able to power five lightbulbs. The first geothermal power plant

Geothermal plants either use steam directly from the earth, or they use hot water from the earth to make steam within the plant.

Hot springs or geysers often occur in geothermal hotspots.

was built in Italy in 1911. That plant is still in use today and can power approximately 1 million homes.

More than 20 countries now use geothermal energy. The United States is the world's largest producer. Geothermal energy is easiest to make when heat is near the earth's surface. However, some wells are drilled up to one mile (1.6 km) deep. They can tap into deep underground supplies of steam and hot water.

3 million
Number of Americans using geothermal energy.

- Introduced by Piero Ginori Conti in 1904.
- Produces little pollution.
- Available day and night, year-round, unlike other renewable energy sources.
- Difficult to access in some areas.

17

DEMAND FOR SOLAR ENERGY HEATS UP

The sun provides heat and light. That makes it a good source of natural power. Scientists have been trying to use solar power since the Industrial Revolution in the 1800s. Some scientists were already worried about running out of fossil fuels. A few thought solar power could be a solution.

Auguste Mouchout, a math teacher in France, made one breakthrough. In 1860, he put an iron pot filled

IN THE MIDDLE OF NOWHERE

Solar panels can provide electricity to buildings in remote areas far from power plants. A solar panel is cheaper and safer than using kerosene lamps or candles. Millions of homes in Asia and Africa use solar panels for power. Solar panels can also power schools and health clinics in remote areas.

Many homeowners install solar panels to generate electricity for their own use.

One criticism of solar power is that fields of panels create an eyesore.

with water inside a glass frame. Warm sunlight passed through the glass and heated the pot. The water boiled, making steam. It did not produce enough steam to be a power source. So Mouchout added a reflector to focus the sun's rays. With that, he made a working steam engine using solar power.

Another breakthrough came a century later. American inventor Alvin Marks patented two types of solar panels in 1988. He coated glass panels with millions of tiny metal strips. When sunlight hits the strips, the energy is transferred to the metal. It is then converted to electricity. In 2013, six of the 10 largest homebuilders in the United States offered solar panels as an option on new houses. Smaller solar panels can power devices such as calculators.

2

Percentage of energy provided by solar in the United States.

- Auguste Mouchout made a working steam engine using solar power in the 1860s.
- Alvin Marks patented solar panels in 1988.
- Renewable energy source, produces little pollution.

WIND TURBINES TURN INTO BIG POWER SOURCE

Windmills have been used for thousands of years to make energy. Wind turns the windmill blades. This energy could be used to pump water and grind grain. But before the 1800s, this power could not be stored for use on less windy days. And the energy could not be sent far away.

Large windmills can now make electricity that can be stored or sent long distances. These large windmills are called wind turbines. In 1888, Charles F. Brush was the first person to use one. He built a 60-foot (18.3-m) tall iron tower in his backyard. The windmill had 144 blades in a wheel 56 feet

Wind turbines have to be built far away from trees or other large objects that would block the wind.

3,464

Number of wind turbines built across the United States in 2011.

- Introduced by Charles F. Brush in 1888 in Ohio.
- Renewable resource, does not cause pollution.
- Costs about the same as coal and gas power.
- Provides less than 1 percent of US power.

(17.1 m) across. The spinning wheel turned pulleys and belts. They were connected to more than 400 batteries in Brush's basement.

THINK ABOUT IT

Many people worked on each energy breakthrough. Why does it take so many people to create new technologies? Why does it take so many years? Is there more work to do in the future?

He powered hundreds of lamps and three electric motors with his windmill.

The first wind turbines were not very efficient. That meant power made this way cost a lot. Slowly, over decades, technology improved. The cost of wind power went down. By 2010, wind powered more than 11 million homes.

Each blade on an industrial wind turbine is more than 100 feet (30.5 m) long.

PLANT FUELS ON THE RISE

Ethanol is a fuel made from plants. Plants are a renewable resource, so ethanol is, too. In the United States, most ethanol is made from corn. Other sources include rice, sugarcane, potato skins, yard clippings, and bark. Scientists are also developing other types of plant fuels. Some farmers are trying to make fuel from trees and grass.

In 1826, Samuel Morey made an engine that used ethanol and turpentine. Henry Ford, founder of the Ford motor company, built his first car to run on pure ethanol in 1896. Ford's famous Model T car could run on ethanol, gasoline, or a mix of the two. However, gasoline became the fuel of choice for cars in the 1920s. A small amount of ethanol was often added to gas because it helped engines run better.

Large amounts of land are needed to grow crops for ethanol production.

13 billion

Gallons (49 billion L) of ethanol produced in the United States in 2013.

- Developed by Samuel Morey in 1826 in the United States.
- Renewable fuel made from corn and other plant substances.
- Can be made locally.
- Better engine efficiency than gasoline.

Gasoline/ethanol blends are sometimes called gasohol.

Most cars are not made to run on pure ethanol. Cars that can run on either gasoline or ethanol are called "flexible fuel" cars. In 2005, more than 4 million flexible-fuel vehicles were being driven in the United States. In 2014, more than 1,200 gas stations offered ethanol fuel in the United States, and more ethanol stations are being built. If this trend continues, studies suggest plant fuels could replace 30 percent of US gasoline by 2030.

REDUCING POLLUTION

When cars use ethanol or gasoline fuel, they release carbon dioxide into the air. Carbon dioxide is a greenhouse gas that can affect the earth's climate. But ethanol is made from plants. As the crops grow, the plants take in carbon dioxide and release oxygen. Because of this, using ethanol-based fuels reduces the amount of greenhouse gases in the atmosphere.

HYBRID CARS PROVIDE FUEL-EFFICIENT ALTERNATIVE

Some of the earliest cars used electric power, but they lost popularity to gas cars. People became interested in electric cars again in the 1960s. They were seen as a way to reduce air pollution. Then oil prices rose in the 1970s. Drivers thought electric cars might help them avoid high prices at gas pumps.

In 1972, Victor Wouk built the first full-size hybrid vehicle. Wouk started with a regular car. He put in a different engine along with an electric motor. The car could go up to 85 miles per hour (137 km/h).

A hybrid car uses both gasoline and electricity. The electric motor uses small amounts of energy at low speeds. It does not produce any exhaust, so there is no pollution. However, electric motors do not work well at high speeds or for long distances. This problem is solved

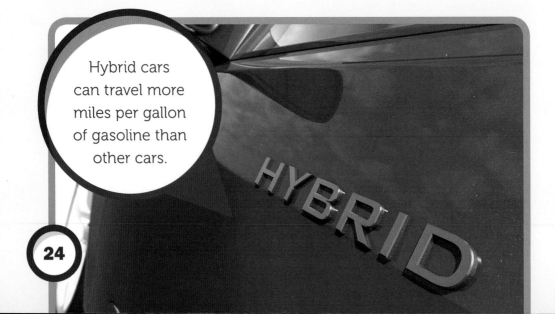

Hybrid cars can travel more miles per gallon of gasoline than other cars.

In a hybrid car, an electric motor provides some of the power, so the gasoline engine is smaller.

1 million
Number of hybrid cars predicted to be produced each year by 2020.

- Invented by Victor Wouk in 1972 in the United States.
- The most fuel-efficient of all cars.
- Less polluting than gas-only cars.

by having a second motor that uses gasoline. Gasoline engines work better at high speeds. They can also charge the electric battery if it gets low.

Years passed before hybrid cars were widely available. In 1997, the hybrid Toyota Prius came out in Japan. In the first year, 18,000 of the cars sold. Other companies started selling hybrid cars. Approximately 90,000 hybrid cars were sold in 2013.

HYDROGEN FUEL CELLS COULD POWER THE FUTURE

To reduce pollution caused by gasoline engines, scientists keep looking for better ways to power cars. One option is the hydrogen fuel cell. General Electric first developed these fuel cells in the 1950s. They were used by NASA to power several space flight missions in the 1960s.

A fuel cell is similar to a battery. But a battery loses power as it is used. It must then be thrown away or recharged. A fuel cell uses a chemical process to make electricity. It will keep making electricity as long as it has a fuel supply.

Several companies have started testing cars that use the hydrogen fuel cell.

This hydrogen-powered race car competed in a race in France in 2013.

40

Number of hydrogen fueling stations planned to be built by 2015.

- Developed by General Electric in the 1950s.
- Used to power space missions in the 1960s.
- Produces less pollution than gasoline cars.
- Fuel can be made from renewable sources.

A hydrogen fuel cell uses oxygen and hydrogen as fuel. Oxygen is found in the air. Hydrogen can be found in water or plants. That means this fuel can be made from renewable sources. Also, this fuel does not make a lot of pollution.

The first hydrogen fuel cell cars were expected to go on sale in 2015. Before they are widely used, hydrogen fueling stations will need to be built in more places.

FACT SHEET

- Coal, natural gas, and nuclear are the most-used energy sources in the United States. But the use of coal has been shrinking. Coal produced approximately 40 percent of our electricity in 2014. This is down from almost 50 percent a decade earlier. Renewable energy sources are growing. They still make up only a small part of our energy use. Approximately 9 percent of US power use came from renewable energy in 2014.

- The use of fossil fuels creates pollution. Renewable energy is better for the planet. But even renewable energy can cause problems. For example, wind turbines can kill birds and bats. Studies have shown how to reduce these deaths. The wind farms must be put in the right place. Radar could tell when large birds are near and shut down or slow the turbines. High-pitched sounds can drive bats away from the area. It may not be possible to stop every death. But birds and bats can also be killed by fossil fuel power plants.

- Different types of power work best in different areas. Solar power works best in sunny areas. Wind power needs strong, steady winds. Hydroelectric power needs a large source of water. Geothermal power needs hot water underground.

- Governments pass laws about energy. Some are to reduce pollution. One US law requires a small amount of ethanol to be used in gasoline. This reduces pollution from cars. Other laws are for safety. Many people have died in coal mining accidents. A 2006 US law helped make coal mines safer. The US government also sets fuel efficiency standards for cars. This requires car manufacturers to make vehicles that use less fuel. New standards passed in 2012 required car manufacturers to double the average fuel efficiency of new cars by 2025.

- Developing a new form of energy is expensive. It takes many years of research. During that time, a company may lose money. Building new power plants is also expensive. Government support can help. Governments sometimes fund research.

GLOSSARY

atom
A basic unit of matter.

efficient
Working well with little wasted effort.

energy
Available power.

engine
A machine using power.

fossil fuel
A fuel made from dead plants or animals, such as coal or oil.

hydrogen
A chemical element that has no color or smell.

Industrial Revolution
A fast change in the economy due to new machinery introduced in the late 1800s.

machine
A piece of equipment with moving parts that uses power.

meltdown
An accident in which a nuclear reactor overheats and releases radiation.

pollution
The release of harmful substances.

radiation
A dangerous form of energy produced during nuclear reactions.

renewable energy
Energy that comes from a source that will not run out, such as the sun or wind.

turbine
A machine for producing power that includes a wheel or rotor.

FOR MORE INFORMATION

Books

Challoner, Jack. *Energy*. New York: DK Children, 2012.

Miller, Debra A. *Energy Production & Alternative Energy*. Farmington Hills, MI: Greenhaven Press, 2010.

Oxlade, Chris. *Nuclear Energy*. Chicago: Heinemann, 2012.

Rigsby, Mike. *Doable Renewables: 16 Alternative Energy Projects for Young Scientists*. Chicago: Chicago Review Press, 2010.

Weakland, Mark. *Onion Juice, Poop, and Other Surprising Sources of Alternative Energy*. North Mankato, MN: Fact Finders, 2011.

Websites

Energy.gov: Science Education
energy.gov/science-innovation/science-education

Energy Kids
www.eia.gov/kids

Kids Energy Zone
www.kidsenergyzone.com

INDEX

About the Author

M. M. Eboch writes about science, history, and culture for all ages. Her novels for young people include historical fiction, ghost stories, and action-packed adventures.